D1378281

Night Diving, Underwater Navigation, and Limited Visibility Diving

by
Steven M. Barsky

SCUBA DIVING
INTERNATIONAL

Published by
International Training, Inc.
Topsham, Maine

Night Diving, Underwater Navigation, and Limited Visibility Diving
by Steven M. Barsky

Scuba Diving International
18 Elm Street
Topsham, ME 04086
Tel: 207-729-4201
FAX: 207-729-4453

Find us on the World Wide Web at http://www.tdisdi.com/

Photography
Principal photography by Bret Gilliam. ©Bret Gilliam. All rights reserved. Additional photography by Steven M. Barsky and Wayne Hasson.
Primary photo models: Lynn Hendrickson, Cathryn Castle, Gretchen Gilliam, George Stuart, Kristine Barsky, Rob Barrel, Dave Merrill, Lenny and Cara Kolczynski.

Illustrations:
© Steven M. Barsky. All rights reserved.

Printed by Ojai Printing, Ojai, CA

ISBN Number: 1-931451-01-X

Library of Congress Control Number: 2001089001

Other Titles Available from Scuba Diving International

Training Manual for Scuba Diving: Dive Training for the 21st Century
Easy Nitrox Diving
Deeper Diving with Dive Computers
Wreck Diving and Boat Diving Techniques
Rescue Diving Manual: A Guide to Rescue Techniques, Stress, Injury, and Accident Management
Dry Suit Diving
Solo Diving Techniques: A Manual for Independent Diving Skills
Visual Inspection Procedures: A Manual for Cylinder Safety
CPROX: Guidelines for Essential CPR and Oxygen Administration
CPR-FIRST: A Concise Manual for Emergency First Aid and CPR

Other Titles Available from Technical Diving International

Nitrox Diver Manual
Advanced Nitrox Diver Manual
Decompression Procedures
Semi-Closed Circuit Rebreather Manual: Draeger Units
Trimix Diving Manual
Extended Range Diver Manual
Cave and cavern Diving Manual
Advanced Wreck Diving
Deep Diving: An Advanced Guide to Physiology, Procedures, and Systems
Nitrox Blending Manual: Guide to Preparation of Oxygen Enriched Air
Advanced Gas Blending Manual: Nitrox, Trimix, and Custom Mixes

WARNING!

Night diving is an activity that places the diver in the underwater environment at times when there is little or no available light from the surface. In this type of diving, the diver is almost entirely dependent on hand-held lights that he carries with him underwater. Because the diver is heavily dependent on artificial light, this situation creates additional risks in addition to the ordinary risks of diving. These risks include difficulty reading instruments, buddy separation, entanglement, failure of dive lights, the failure of boat operators to see divers, disorientation, and becoming lost in fog. These risks can lead to personal injury or death.

Diving in limited visibility is similar to night diving and poses many of the same risks as night diving. In limited visibility diving, however, a dive light is often of little or no use in providing supplementary illumination. Buddy separation and entanglement are the two greatest risks of limited visibility diving. If the diver cannot free himself and his buddy is unavailable to lend assistance, the diver may run out of air and drown.

Limited visibility may be caused by contaminants in the water that may pose a threat to the diver's health and life. If the diver is uncertain as to the cause of limited visibility he is advised not to dive. However, contaminants are not always obvious and even water that appears to be "clean" may contain bacteria or other organisms that pose a threat to the safety of the diver. Diving in contaminated water requires specialized training, equipment, and experience that is beyond the scope of this book.

This book is designed as a source of information to help the diver avoid problems that may be encountered in night and limited visibility diving. However, only through acquiring the right equipment, proper training, and experience can the diver become prepared to engage in these activities.

Table of Contents

Table of Contents

Foreword

Bret Gilliam, CEO Scuba Diving Intnl.

This book takes on three subjects that are all related. Night diving is a unique experience for divers, allowing them to visit the underwater world and view the environment from a different perspective. Some marine life normally active during the day are asleep or inactive. Other forms of life have just begun their activity cycles and can be observed feeding or tending to their habitat under the cloak of darkness. The ocean is a fascinating new place at night - particularly if the diver begins his dive at sunset when the nocturnal population stirs into action just as the typical "day trippers" are seeking shelter.

While most divers feel a bit of apprehension upon entering the water at night, this feeling quickly gives way to the excitement of experiencing the night reef and all its wonders. Creatures that are never seen during the day come out in full splendor for the observer with a simple underwater light as his guide. Octopus, lobster, crabs, and many fish are wary during the day but lose their inhibitions once the sun has set. The night diver is privileged to be introduced to a whole new population of critters and corals blooming on the night reef.

Night diving also requires a bit of expertise in finding your way around when standard daylight disappears. This is also true of water lacking the clarity of the tropics, where the basic elements of navigation become so important.

Daniel Boone, the great woodsman and pioneer, was once asked if he had ever been lost. He replied, "No, but I was damn confused there for about two weeks once." Boone may well have made a good diver, but I'd like to think we could have helped him a bit finding his way around.

The underwater environment can be a tricky place even in the best of conditions. But when you add in the complexities of limited visibility or diving at night, swimming in a weightless state without traditional references is enough to confuse anyone.

We asked longtime dive professional Steve Barsky to craft a book that would help you overcome the obstacles and show you how easy it really can be to reliably find your way both underwater and topside. You'll see that divers have many tools to help navigate including such natural aids as sand ripples or reef formations that accurately predict your route. Mechanical compasses have been around for years and Barsky helps unravel the practical skills and techniques to use them effectively. He also explains the new technologies at our fingertips now including electronic compasses with imbedded memory functions that can automatically make you a more proficient navigator.

Since underwater there is no place to stop and ask directions, we hope that this book will be a valued reference to make sure you end up where you wanted to and come back safely.

Bret Gilliam
President and CEO
SCUBA DIVING INTERNATIONAL

Acknowledgements

I've always had a good sense of direction, whether on the surface or underwater, but I also know how easy it is to get lost. Since I first started diving in 1965, I've had the opportunity to use many different types of navigational equipment and systems, both aboard boats and underwater.

This book represents the diving experiences I have had the good fortune to enjoy all over the world, in many different diving environments. We all learn how to become better underwater navigators each time we dive. Many thanks to my dive partners who have shared their tricks for navigation with me.

Numerous people have provided the assistance necessary to make this book possible. Special thanks goes to the following folks:

- Rob Arnold, Atlanta Swim and Scuba Academy
- Harry Averill with Dive-Rite
- Brian Carney at TDI/SDI Headquarters
- Jim Clymer at AquaLung/Seaquest
- Lucien D'Hondt, Xios Diving Technology
- Larry Elsevier, Cochran Consulting
- Ron Grzelka, Atlanta Swim and Scuba Academy
- Wayne Hasson, Aggressor Fleet
- Lynn Hendrickson at TDI/SDI Headquarters
- Cliff Simoneau
- Jamie Spicer at Scubapro/Uwatec
- John Wall, The Dive Shop

In each of the books for the Scuba Diving International Advanced Diver series we have tried to present diving techniques as people practice them in the real world. We hope you will use this book to discover new dive sites and adventures.

Steven M. Barsky
Santa Barbara, CA

Chapter 1
Never Be Lost Underwater!

Night diving is one of the greatest underwater adventures you can experience. It is a glimpse into a different world, like a reverse reflection of what you normally see underwater, almost like a negative of a photograph. The underwater world looks different at night and many of the animals that inhabit it behave differently.

In night diving you focus down to the area illuminated by your dive light. Around you is blackness, but the colors of the underwater world leap out in the brilliance of your dive light.

In colder waters, small creatures like squid may fill the waters by the millions at night. In warmer waters, tiny marine "worms" may spin madly in front of your lights. Fish sleep while lobsters roam out in the open.

To night dive with confidence, you also need to understand the techniques of underwater navigation. Once you understand underwater navigation and night diving, you are prepared to begin to develop your ability to dive in limited visibility conditions.

Underwater navigation is the key to most diving adventures, because without this skill it is often difficult or impossible to return to a precise location again. Let's take a look at a couple of diving adventures

Night Diving

For the purposes of this course, night diving is any dive that is made more than 30 minutes after sunset or more than 30 minutes before sunrise. Many people have a concern about diving after dark because they think that it will be pitch black underwater and that they won't be able to see the "gotcha" that's lying in wait for them on the bottom. This is a natural concern. However, the reality is that there is always some light underwater at night, unless it is totally overcast, and dive lights shine brightly enough to reveal that there are no "monsters under the reef." Even without a dive light on a night dive you can almost always see, once your eyes grow accustomed to the dark, it's just that there is a total absence of color, not light.

You will use underwater navigation techniques during your night and limited visibility training dives.

One of the best ways to experience night diving for the first time is to enter the water at twilight, when the sun is down, but before it is completely dark. As the remaining daylight fades, you'll see certain animals disappear, while others shake the sleep from their eyes and the "night shift" animals come alive. As the water grows gradually darker, you'll become so engrossed in the sea life around you that you might not even notice that the natural light has gone.

Night diving provides an opportunity to observe many creatures that are not normally seen during daytime dives, as well as to observe interesting behaviors in creatures that act totally different after the sun has set. Night diving is a type of diving adventure that can be enjoyed almost anywhere you might explore underwater. It is an eerie experience the first time you descend into the blackness of a night dive, but your dive light will quickly help you see the spectacular colors of the reef at night.

Limited Visibility Diving

Although there is no precise definition of "limited visibility," we will define limited visibility underwater as any time when you cannot see objects that are more than six feet away from you while you are underwater.

Limited visibility diving is not something that most people want to do, but there may be times during your diving excursions where you need or want to dive under conditions where the visibility is limited. Limited visibility diving is usually done when divers must dive to recover lost objects. In some parts of the world, the water is almost never clear, and if you want to dive you must adapt to the local conditions. While we all would prefer to dive in clear water, there are often interesting things to see and do in water with limited visibility. Underwater navigation techniques are used on all dives, but become especially important if you dive at night or in limited visibility.

The Importance of Underwater Navigation

One of the most frustrating events you can experience in diving is finding a great dive spot on a particular dive, and never being able to locate it again. For a variety of reasons, this happens to divers all of the time. Whether because they are poor at underwater navigation, diving in limited visibility, or diving at night, divers regularly discover great diving sites, only to "lose" them and be unable to locate them again.

When the sun goes down, lobsters come out of their holes to feed at night.

Underwater navigation can be defined as any technique that a diver uses underwater to travel from a one point to another. The diver who is proficient in underwater navigation is able to swim from his starting point to a desired target and return to his original starting point without surfacing.

In this book, we're going to share the secrets of underwater navigation with you, so that you'll be able to effectively locate and relocate any underwater site on a consistent basis. Even if you only dive in clear water, the secrets of underwater navigation will help you relocate any dive spot and increase your underwater efficiency, safety, and enjoyment.

There are many different techniques and devices that you can use to help you navigate underwater. Aside from the simple, but reliable mechanical compass, there are natural navigation techniques, as well as many different types of electronics that can help you navigate with ease underwater. This book will explain the many different options that are available to make your underwater navigation more successful.

Developing Your Underwater Navigation, Night, and Limited Visibility Diving Skills

During these courses, you will learn how to perform the following:

- Explain how a compass works and the different features of the compass.
- Use and recover an underwater marker buoy.
- Use natural navigation to assist you in diving a site and returning to your starting point underwater.
- Use a mechanical or electronic compass to swim a straight course and return to your starting point underwater.
- Use a mechanical or electronic compass to swim a "box" course, consisting of three 90-degree turns, to return to your starting point underwater.
- Use triangulation on the surface to return to a dive site underwater.
- Plan and perform a dive at night.
- Plan and perform a dive in limited visibility.

You'll probably start out by learning underwater navigation during daytime dives so that you can use these skills effectively at night. Once you've mastered underwater navigation and night diving, you'll be ready to progress to the limited visibility experience.

How to Use this Book

This book will be a reference for you to use during these specialty courses. It is essential for you to read and understand all of the information in this book. If any of the material in this book is unclear to you, please discuss the concepts with your instructor so that you understand all of the information. It is essential for you to understand how to navigate properly underwater and effectively dive at night and in limited visibility.

Don't hesitate to take this book with you on your openwater diving trips to refresh your understanding of the concepts explained in this text.

Scuba I.Q. Review

At the end of each chapter of this book we will present a series of review questions that your SDI diving instructor will discuss with you. You must understand each concept and technique in order to navigate underwater, as well as to effectively dive at night and in limited visibility.

1) List two methods that can be used to navigate underwater.

2) Define the term "night diving."

3) Define the term "limited visibility diving."

Chapter 2
Equipment for Night Diving, Underwater Navigation & Limited Visibility Diving

Underwater navigation is a skill that you will use on every dive and not just an end to itself. To be a good diver, you must be successful at underwater navigation. Good navigation skills will take you where you want to go, to do the things you want to do. Similarly, night and limited visibility diving skills will help you achieve the things you want to do underwater.

To navigate underwater, or make night or limited visibility dives, you will need some additional pieces of gear beyond what you may already own. These items include a compass, an underwater light, a slate, a marker buoy, and other devices. You will find that you will use these items during the course and throughout your diving experience. Additional items that may be useful are discussed elsewhere in the text.

The Mechanical Underwater Compass

The compass is one of the oldest navigational devices in the world, and one of the simplest to use. With a simple compass and good navigation skills you can travel almost anywhere.

A compass is a device used for navigation, both topside and underwater. The compass consists of a non-magnetic case which is filled with oil. Inside the case there is a magnetized card (or needle) that points toward the magnetic north pole of the Earth. No matter which way you turn, as long as the compass is held level horizontally, it will always point towards the magnetic north pole. The card has the four points of the compass printed on it, i.e., north, south, east, and west. In addition, it also has divisions along the edge of the card, known as "degree marks" printed on it. Since the compass card is round, the circle is divided into 360 degrees.

You view the compass card through a lens on the top of the case. On the top of the lens there is a permanent line that is etched, painted, or molded

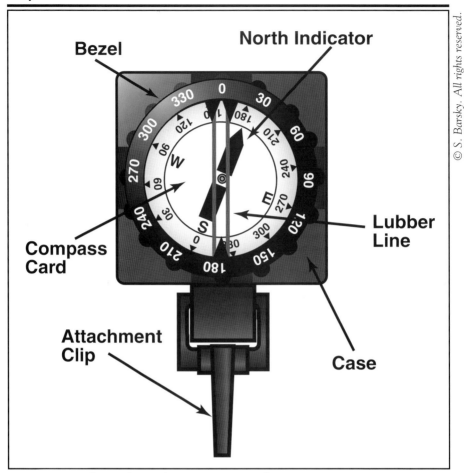

The mechanical compass is a simple instrument to use.

into it. This line is known as the "lubber line." On the outside of the case is a rotating plastic ring known as a "bezel," that also has degrees painted or inscribed on it.

You can purchase an underwater compass with a variety of mounting options. They can be mounted on your console with your other instruments. Wrist models are preferred by some divers, while others choose to wear theirs attached to their buoyancy compensator, using a spring loaded retractor. We'll explore the advantages and disadvantages of different methods of mounting your compass in the chapter on underwater navigation techniques.

Underwater compasses are usually made from rugged plastic. They will withstand a great deal of abuse, but should be treated with respect and care. A simple rinse with fresh water at the end of your diving day is usually all the maintenance most compasses require.

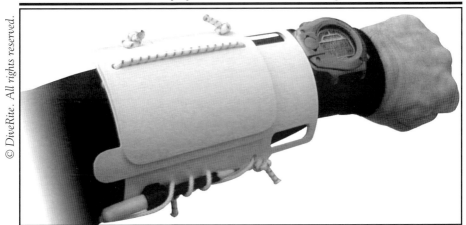

A slate is a necessity if you are serious about relocating dive sites.

Take Notes on Your Slate

A slate is an indispensible piece of gear for all diving, but is particularly useful for activities like underwater navigation and photography. It is handy for taking notes and for communicating with your buddy underwater.

For dives where you are practicing underwater navigation techniques, a slate is essential for writing down compass courses, recording natural navigation features of the underwater terrain, and for triangulation, a technique for relocating dive sites.

If you use a flat slate, it can be attached to your buoyancy compensator, or stored in a pocket on your wetsuit or dry suit. Some divers also use round slates, that fit over their sleeves.

To clean a slate after you have written on it, run fresh water on the slate and sprinkle it with an abrasive cleaner, such as Ajax®, and rub it with an abrasive sponge. You can also erase any marks on the slate using an ordinary eraser. Either way, the slate is ready to go back in the water immediately.

Marker Buoys

There are many different types of marker buoys available that are useful in marking a dive site or for practicing your underwater navigation skills. You can also make a simple buoy from items that are commonly available.

The two main categories of commercially available buoys for scuba diving are inflatable buoys and rigid buoys. Both types work well.

Inflatable buoys consist of some type of soft bladder, similar to a balloon. Two advantages of inflatable buoys are that they can be rolled up for storage and transport and inflated only when needed. A line is fastened to the buoy

This marker buoy is well designed and easy to use.

You can make your own marker buoy from a plastic bottle.

Inflatable marker buoys are also available.

on one end and to the object to be marked on the other end.

Rigid buoys are made from either hard plastic or from a non-compressible foam material. A small weight is usually attached to this type of buoy to offset its buoyancy and to serve as an anchor for the bottom end. Rigid buoys do not require any inflation and are not prone to puncture. This type of buoy can be a bit more bulky to carry than the inflatable buoy.

To make a simple buoy for marking a dive site from the surface, you can use an old plastic bottle, with nylon line appropriate to the water depth, and a two or three pound weight to anchor the buoy. However, homemade devices tend to be less reliable and more difficult to use.

In the next chapter, you'll learn techniques for using underwater marking buoys.

Dive Lights

A dive light is one of the first accessories that many divers buy after their certification course. They're not only useful at night, they're also handy during the day, especially on deeper dives to help restore the colors filtered out by the water. In California, most lobster divers carry lights even on daytime dives to help them look into holes and crevices while hunting for lobsters.

Dive lights differ from ordinary topside flashlights in that they have waterproof and pressure-proof cases and switches. They are much more rugged and usually heavier than typical flashlights. Most dive lights today are made from either plastic or machined aluminum.

As battery and bulb technology have improved, dive lights have gotten smaller and smaller over the years. Although you might think a large light would provide more power and light, this isn't necessarily true. Many of the smaller dive lights available today provide more than adequate light without the need for additional bulk or weight. In most cases, the smaller the light you can use, the better.

Any light you select for night diving should be a non-floating light, or should be easily weighted so that it will sink. Non-floating lights are preferred because if you need to set your light down on the bottom, you don't want it to float away. If your light floats to the surface, and there is any surface swell or wind waves, you will probably lose your light.

Dive lights must be both water-proof and pressure-proof.

Dive lights need not be large to be effective.

Besides the traditional hand-held light, there are also head-mounted lights that provide a good alternative for night diving. Head-mounted lights are an excellent choice for the underwater photographer or hunter.

Every hand-held dive light should be equipped with a lanyard so that it can be worn on your wrist or attached to your dive gear. However, you must be able to easily remove the light in the event you need to remove it quickly in an emergency.

For night diving, it is recommended that you carry a minimum of two lights. They do not both need to be the same size. One light is used as your primary light and the second is used as your back-up light in case the first one fails.

Each manufacturer has different recommendations for the care and maintenance of their lights, so be sure to check the literature provided with each individual light. The general maintenance procedure is to rinse or soak the light in fresh, clean water after every use. Allow the light to dry out of the sun, or wipe it dry with a towel.

Once the light is dry, open the battery compartment to avoid permanent compression of the sealing o-ring. On most modern lights, opening the battery compartment requires that you unscrew the lens or "head" of the light. You need not leave the light open, but the lens should be unscrewed to the point where the o-ring is no longer compressed. Just be sure to screw the lens closed before you dive with the light again or it will flood!

If you will not be diving again for some time, remove the batteries from the light to avoid damage to the mechanism in the event the batteries leak. One caution that should be observed with any dive light, however, is to avoid leaving it in the sun in hot weather as the heat can cause the batteries to swell and leak. Also, some dive lights run much hotter than ordinary topside flashlights and should not be used out of the water, except for brief periods.

Light Sticks and Marker Lights

In addition to your dive light, you will also need several other specially designed lights for use while night diving. These include light sticks and marker lights.

Light sticks are small lights that are designed to attach to a diver's snorkel or tank valve to identify their location, both on the surface and underwater. Chemical light sticks are available that are relatively inexpensive. These devices consist of a heavy walled plastic tube with an inner cylinder of thin glass. The outer plastic tube and the inner thin walled glass tube contain two different chemicals. Chemical light sticks are also known as "cyalumes."

When the plastic tube is bent, the glass tube breaks and the chemicals mix together. Once the chemicals mix, they emit a bright glow that lasts for several hours. Chemical light sticks can be attached to a diver's snorkel using waterproof electrical tape, or tied to the tank valve or regulator first stage using a bit of string. In recent years, chemical light sticks have lost their popularity with some divers who feel they are not as environmentally friendly or economical as reusable battery powered light sticks.

Battery powered light sticks are also available and these work well, too. These devices function like a small flashlight, except that the bulb is encased in a plastic shroud that is completely transparent, so the light can be seen from any angle. Battery powered light sticks are reusable by simply replacing the batteries when they lose power or the bulb when it burns out. If you night dive on a regular basis, a battery powered light stick is more economical than a disposable chemical light.

Marker lights or "exit lights" are used to help you relocate the anchor line underwater if you are diving from a boat, or to help you relocate your entry point if you are diving from the beach. There are many different types

Marking lights can be either chemical, like the one on the bottom, or battery powered, like the two upper lights.

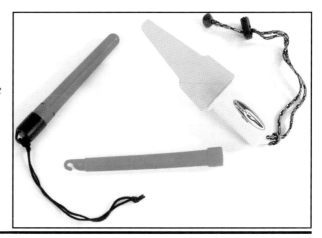

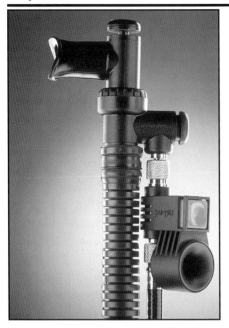

Some type of sound signalling device is essential for night diving. You can use a whistle or an air-powered horn like this one. (© Ideations. All rights reserved.)

of marker lights that work well, but it's a good idea to pick something distinctive, like a strobe or a light with a colored lens, that is easy to identify compared to any other lights that may surround it.

Sound Signalling Devices

For all diving, it is strongly recommended that you carry some type of sound signalling device for getting the attention of the boat operator if you are swept away by a current and your light is not working. For night diving this is essential. This can be a whistle or an air powered horn that works off the low-pressure air from your regulator.

Retractors

Retractors are small spring-loaded mechanical reels that are used to attach dive accessories to your buoyancy compensator. They can be used to attach lights, gauges, slates, and other accessories. When you pull the accessory away from your body, the retractor unspools the line and when you release the accessory, the retractor automatically reels it back in out of your way. Retractors are invaluable accessories for carrying your spare dive light or slate.

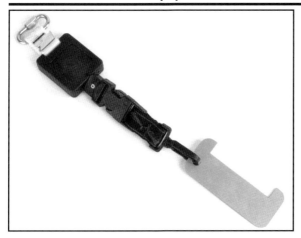

This lobster measuring gauge (bottom) is attached to a retractor.

Electronic Navigation Aids

The number of electronic aids that can assist you in underwater navigation continues to grow each year and their capabilities are astonishing. The most popular electronic aids are dive tracking devices, electronic compasses, and underwater sonar. For divers who need extremely precise locating capabilities, underwater GPS (Global Positioning System) is also available. Although underwater GPS systems are currently priced out of the range of most sport divers, no doubt they will be commonly available in the future.

Dive tracking devices are designed to help you relocate the boat or a site that you have marked. The system consists of two devices; a sending unit that emits an electronic signal, and an electronic receiver. The sending unit can be hung over the side of the boat, attached to the anchor line, or attached to a wreck or other underwater site. As long as the sending unit is on and has battery power, it gives out a continuous directional signal that can only be picked up by the receiver.

This is the receiving unit for an underwater tracking system.

Electronic compasses are highly accurate and easy to use.

To use the receiving unit, the diver turns on the receiver and swings the unit as he turns in a circle. When the receiver is pointing directly towards the sending unit, the display indicates the correct direction and distance. These are very simple units to use and they make underwater navigation extremely simple.

Electronic compasses extend the capability of the ordinary mechanical compass. They perform course calculations for you automatically, and are much more precise than traditional mechanical compasses.

Underwater sonar units are used primarily to measure distances to large objects in limited visibility. These systems are helpful in locating wrecks and reefs.

The Global Positioning System, or "GPS" as it is more popularly known, is a system designed by the U.S. military, using satellites to help locate positions on earth. A series of satellites in orbit around the earth each send out a signal that can be picked up by GPS receivers. The receivers interpret the signal from each satellite and by mathematical calculation, provide the location of the receiver.

When people say they own a GPS they actually mean they own a GPS receiver. GPS receivers are widely used topside, and are quite inexpensive and simple to use. You may have the opportunity during your navigation course to see how GPS operates, particularly if you do any of your diving from a boat.

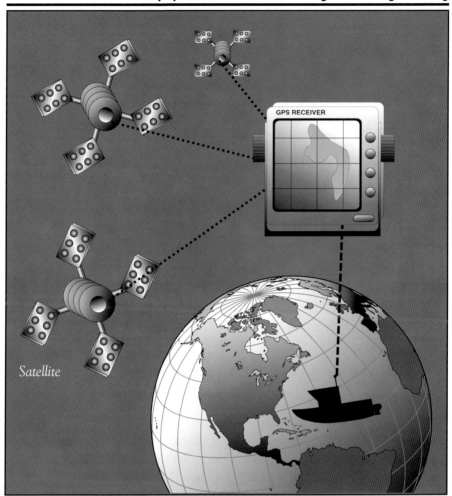

Satellite

The Global Positioning System uses satellites in space to help locate objects and places on earth. Each of the satellites transmits a signal that is "heard" by the receiver aboard the boat. By measuring the distance to each of the satellites, the receiver calculates the position of the boat. GPS is a tremendous aid to navigation.

Some dive boats are still equipped with LORAN, which is an acronym that stands for Long Range Navigational system. LORAN is a good system that has been used for many years and also provides accurate navigational information. LORAN works in a similar fashion to the GPS system, but the transmitting stations for the LORAN system are located on land rather than in space.

Divers use LORAN and GPS systems in conjunction with a depth finder (fathometer) to position themselves on a dive site. Once the boat is anchored close to the correct spot, depending on the size of the site, you may still need to search for it underwater.

Full-Face Masks and Wireless Communications

Two additional items that can be of tremendous value in many diving activities, but especially in night and limited visibility diving are a full-face mask and wireless communications. The full-face mask is a diving mask that covers the eyes, nose, and mouth. Wireless communications are electronic devices that capture human speech, transmit them through the water as an electronic signal, and reconvert them to a sound you can hear. These two pieces of gear, working together, will allow you to communicate without the need to see your dive partner face-to-face. In certain situations, this type of equipment could save your life.

Full-face masks are not difficult to use, but they do require some additional training before you can use one properly in open water. Ask your instructor about additional training in this specialized equipment.

A full-face mask with communications will allow you to talk to other divers who are similarly equipped. This type of equipment is extremely useful in limited visibility.

Scuba I.Q. Review

The equipment you will use during this course is gear that you can use throughout your diving career. Discuss your gear selection with your instructor by reviewing the following questions.

1) List four parts of the mechanical compass.

2) List two ways that a diver can wear a compass.

3) Describe two ways to erase marks from an underwater slate.

4) State the two different types of marker buoys and list one advantage of each.

5) Explain why a non-floating dive light is preferred to a floating light.

6) Explain why night divers always carry a minimum of two lights underwater.

7) State the function of a retractor.

8) List three types of electronic underwater navigation devices.

Chapter 3
Using Marker Buoys

Marker buoys are incredibly useful devices that can play a big part in helping you relocate a dive site. Temporarily marking a site will allow you to easily return for a second dive on the same day without the need to use any navigation skills. By temporarily marking the site, you'll also be able to easily take topside bearings that will allow you to return to the same site again and again. You'll learn how to take topside bearings and use a technique known as "triangulation" in Chapter 5 of this book.

Placing the Marker Buoy

In setting marker buoys, divers seem to have the most difficulty with managing the line that connects the buoy to the anchor (or weight) that holds the buoy in location. It is not uncommon for divers to have the line become tangled in their gear. Careful handling of the buoy and a bit of practice will help you prevent this from happening.

Before you use a commercially available buoy for the first time, take a good look at how it is put together, how the line is coiled, and how the line connects to the buoy. You need to understand exactly how the buoy works before you take it underwater so that you can set it properly in the minimum

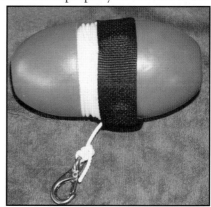

Whatever type of buoy you use must be properly rigged before you take it in the water.

Once you release the buoy, it will start to reel out towards the surface.

amount of time and so you can recover it easily without ending up with a line tangled in knots. It is also helpful to mark the line with a magic marker, starting at the anchor end, so that you know how much line is in the water. You can mark the line by writing on it with the marker every ten feet. One mark indicates 10 feet, two marks indicate 20 feet, three marks indicate thirty feet, and so on.

If you drop the anchor from the buoy from the surface to mark a site, unless the water is extremely clear and/or shallow, you probably won't be able to see where the anchor has landed on the bottom. If the anchor has landed in sand, it is possible that the buoy will move if there is a strong current or wind. You'll want to anchor the buoy to a fixed object, such as part of a wreck, a rock, or a dead piece of coral, as soon as possible.

You can fasten the buoy to a stationery object by tying a simple overhand knot or using a brass snaphook on the anchor end. Avoid fastening the buoy to living corals because they can be easily damaged.

Most commercially manufactured marker buoys have lots of line on them to allow you to mark sites in deep water. You need to be familiar with how to fasten the line off so that it doesn't all unspool. If you use buoys regularly within a set of particular depth ranges you may want to own more than one buoy with the line trimmed on each for different diving depths.

You must take most of the slack out of the buoy line if you plan to use the topside location of the buoy to take your bearings for triangulation (see Chapter 5). If there is too much line in the water the buoy will not be directly over the spot you are trying to mark and any bearings that you take based on its location will be inaccurate. In addition, excess line creates a hazard that you can become entangled in and increases the chances that the buoy will be snagged by a passing boat.

If you are marking a location while you are underwater, fasten the end of the buoy to a non-moving object before you release the buoy. Uncoil enough line for the water depth in which you are working, allowing for the tidal changes in your area, and tie off the excess line so it does not unravel when you release the buoy to the surface.

Sometimes divers think they have lost buoys because they have not left enough slack in the buoy line and the buoy disappears. If you do not allow enough slack in the buoy to compensate for tidal changes or currents, it is possible for your buoy to be submerged by the rising tide or a strong current. If you're in the right area and don't see the buoy, take a good look around before you assume the buoy is lost. It just might be a few feet below the surface.

Avoiding Entanglement

Ideally, the line supplied with your buoy will float when the buoy is released, so you don't end up with a big ball of line on the bottom. When you deploy the buoy, feed the line out a bit at a time, rather than allowing the buoy to run free. If you marked your line before your dive, release as much line as the depth of water you're in, plus an additional 10 feet to counteract

If you plan to use the buoy for triangulation you must take the slack out of the line.

the effect of waves or current. Feed the buoy out so that it is deployed down current from you, rather than having the buoy coming back towards you.

Recovering the Buoy

Once the buoy has been released from the bottom, the best place to recover your line and the anchor for the buoy is on the surface, There are several reasons for this. First, it is much easier to recover the line with the anchor on the end of it keeping the line taut. Secondly, if you are underwater, there is a greater chance of entanglement with the line as you attempt to reel it in. Finally, there is no reason to waste your bottom time reeling in the line when this can be done on the surface more easily.

For most commercially manufactured buoys, it is important to wrap the buoy line in exactly the same way and with the same tension as it was originally supplied to you to ensure that the buoy line will deploy correctly. If the line is not wrapped tightly enough, or if it is wrapped irregularly, the line will either knot when the buoy is released and/or will release before you intend to use the buoy.

Never leave a buoy on a dive site any longer than is essential. If you are marking a secret dive spot, you run the risk that other divers will discover your site! In addition, a buoy left for an extended period on a dive site may be picked up by another diver as abandoned, even if it is marked with your name.

Never leave a buoy on a dive site any longer than necessary. Rewind the buoy carefully so that it unreels properly the next time you use it.

There is also the risk that a passing boat may accidentally snag the line, fouling their propeller and causing damage to their propulsion unit. You could theoretically be held responsible for expensive repairs if this were to occur.

Practice Using Buoys in Good Conditions

Always practice using a buoy in good conditions, i.e, no current and good visibility before you attempt to use a buoy when conditions are poor. You should be proficient in the use of a buoy before attempting to use one when conditions are challenging.

Scuba I.Q. Review

Using marker buoys will help you to relocate dive sites easily. Buoys can also be a useful tool to help you practice your underwater navigation skills. Discuss these aspects of buoy use with your instructor.

1) Explain why it is recommended to mark a buoy line in 10 foot increments.

2) State two possible factors that can cause a buoy to drift away if it is not anchored to the bottom.

3) Explain why a buoy should not be tied to living coral.

4) State two reasons why it is desirable to avoid having excess line in the water after you have anchored your buoy.

5) Explain why a diver might think their buoy is lost even though it is anchored to the bottom.

6) List two reasons why a buoy line should be recovered on the surface rather than underwater.

7) State two reasons why a buoy should not be left in the water any longer than necessary.

8) List the two conditions that should be present when you initially practice using a buoy.

Chapter 4
Underwater Navigation

On a trip to California, you decide to take in a day of diving at the Channel Islands off Santa Barbara. You and your dive buddy enter the cold, clear water and swim down through the blades of giant kelp as they wave slowly in the current.

A curious harbor seal drifts by, circles you, and seems to invite you to follow him. You snap a few photos with your camera and swim after the seal to try to get a few more pictures.

Along the outer edge of the rocky reef, the seal swims into the enormous opening of an underwater cavern, pokes his head out, and ducks back inside. You and your buddy pull out your dive lights and shine them through the cavern opening. The floor of the cavern is covered with small pebbles and the room is only a few feet deep. But the walls and the ceiling of the cavern are covered with huge lobsters! There are hundreds, perhaps a thousand lobsters, all waving their antennae wildly as the harbor seal swims lazily around the room.

The seal swims out and once he is out of the way, you start taking photographs of the lobsters as they crawl around the cavern. Some of the lobsters walk right up to you, but they quickly scurry away if you reach out to touch them. Pretty soon, there are lobsters whizzing past your face, bouncing off the walls, and climbing over each other. In your excitement, you run through the remainder of your film and your air in a short time. As you swim back to the boat, you realize that you don't know how you will find this spot again. If you knew how to navigate properly underwater, you would probably be able to locate this spot again with ease.

Why Navigation Skills are Important

Good underwater navigation skills not only make your diving more enjoyable; they can also be essential to your safety. For example, if you find yourself in the middle of a thick kelp bed, it is much less fatiguing to be able to navigate back to your starting point underwater, than to attempt to swim across the kelp on the surface. If you dive in areas where there is heavy boat traffic, it is much safer to be able to navigate back to the anchor line rather than to surface away from the boat in the middle of moving watercraft.

You will use your navigation skills during the navigational exercises during this course, as well as on the night and limited visibility dives.

Types of Underwater Navigation

There are several techniques that are commonly used for underwater navigation. They include natural navigation, traditional magnetic compass navigation, and electronic navigation. Depending on where you dive, your dive objective, and the conditions present, you will probably use at least two of these methods, and possibly all three of them, on any given dive.

The more resources that you can use in your navigation, the more successful you will be in reaching your target. It is unwise to depend on a single source of information to navigate underwater.

One of the most important tools that you must use in your navigation is your brain. If your compass says you are headed in the right direction, but your dive computer shows that you are moving into deeper water, but your target is only at 30 feet, stop swimming and figure out what is wrong.

The angle of the sun can be a tremendous aid to navigation. Use as many aids as you can to help you find your way underwater.

Natural Underwater Navigation

Natural navigation is the technique most commonly used by divers, especially in clear water. However, some elements of natural navigation can also be used at night and in limited visibility. Natural navigation aids can be divided into two categories; physical energy navigational aids such as the sun and currents, and physical features of the environment, such as sand ripples, reefs, wrecks, and marine life that is fixed to the bottom.

One of the most basic aids to natural underwater navigation is the angle of the sun. Before you enter the water, check and see the position of the sun relative to shore or the reef. The angle of the sun's rays will remain relatively constant through all but the very longest dives. If the sun is over your left shoulder as you swim in one direction, it should be over your right shoulder as you return to your starting point.

Using the sun works well when the sun is at an angle to the water, but is not effective when the sun is directly overhead at noon. Of course, if you're diving when its cloudy, foggy, or at night, the sun is of no value in assisting your navigation.

Currents underwater can also be useful navigational aids. As you'll recall from your first scuba training, whenever there is a current, we almost always will start our dive into the current. When you have a detectable current moving in one direction, it's easy to orient yourself underwater.

Sand ripples on the bottom usually run parallel to shore and are another aid to natural navigation

Kelp plants will swing in the direction the current is flowing, providing another clue to your course underwater. In this photo, there is no current.

Of course, currents do change direction and you must pay attention to what's happening during the dive and take notice if the direction varies. Your first clue that the current is changing direction will normally occur when the current slacks off or stops completely.

If you're diving in kelp, the kelp will stream out with the current and give you a very definite frame of reference. If you head into the current at the start of your dive, the kelp will be pointing toward you. Provided the current has not changed while you have been underwater, the kelp will be pointing away from you as you return to your starting point at the end of your dive.

If you're diving in the ocean near shore, the ripples in the sand will usu-ally line up parallel to shore. If you swim at a right angle towards the ripples and the water gets shallower, in most cases you will be moving towards shore, unless there is an offshore reef or sandbar. If you swim at a right angle to the ripples and the water gets deeper, you know you are moving away from shore. If you follow the line of the ripples and the water depth stays the same, you are probably swimming parallel to shore.

Features in the underwater terrain, such as reefs or wrecks will provide recognizable "landmarks" that will help you in your underwater navigation. In addition, the curve or slope of the bottom will indicate whether you are moving deeper or shallower along a site. Marine life that is anchored to the bottom, such as large sponges or coral heads will also provide recognizable waypoints to help you identify your route. You may want to note important terrain features on your slate when you fill out your dive log to help you relocate a particular site.

Navigating with a Mechanical Compass

A compass works on the principle of magnetism. A magnetized card or needle floating in oil will align itself so that northern pole of the magnet points towards the magnetic north pole of the earth. No matter which way you turn, the northern pole of the magnetic card will spin until it aligns itself with the magnetic north pole.

To take a bearing on a distant object, you hold the compass in your hand, or wear it on your wrist, so that the "lubber line" of the compass is aligned with the centerline of the length of your body. Look over the top of the compass and line the lubber line up with the object to which you want to swim, such as a buoy, a reef, or a wreck.

Turn the bezel on the outside of the compass until it lines up with the north pointing needle inside the compass. This is the course you want to follow to reach your target.

Your course to return to your starting point, known as the "reciprocal

Set the bezel to "capture" the needle so you can tell if you are off course.

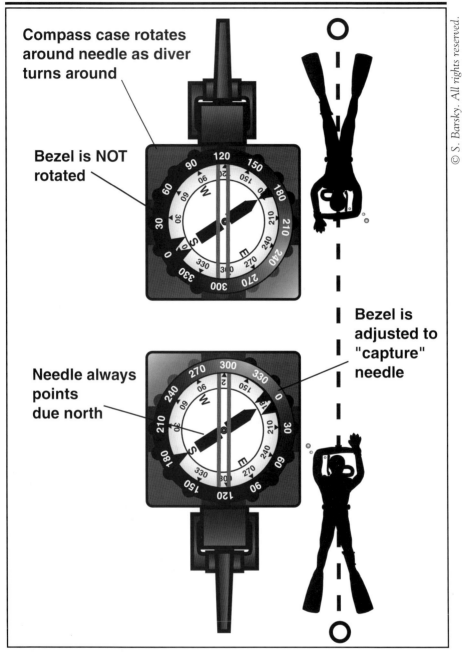

Example of a reciprocal compass course: Staring at the bottom of the page, the diver swims due north. The compass needle always points to north, which in this case is the top of the page. When the diver turns around to head back the way he came, the compass needle still points to north.

course," is 180 degrees out, or directly opposite from your initial course. On the compass on the previous page, the diver started his course with the compass needle pointing between the "V" on the bezel. When he turns around to return to his starting point, the needle still points to north, but the case has rotated around the compass card. The needle now points to the "triangle" on the bezel, directly opposite the "V."

You'll note that if you turn to either side away from where you have the bezel set, the compass card will "swing" away from the point where the bezel is set. In reality, the compass card is not moving, it's still pointing towards north, but the compass case is turning around the card. When this happens you are "off course" and must turn back in the proper direction to reach your heading. Your instructor will have you practice compass exercises on dry land before you attempt to perform them underwater.

Keep in mind that large "ferrous metal objects" can significantly throw off the accuracy of a compass. Ferrous metal objects are any metal item that contains iron, such as the hull of a steel shipwreck. If your underwater navigation takes you near or directly over a shipwreck, the accuracy of your course can be severely affected.

Large metal objects, like shipwrecks, can throw off the accuracy of your compass.

Swimming a Compass Course

To swim a compass course, you hold the compass in the same position that you did when you took your bearing. It is extremely important that you maintain the compass in line with longitudinal axis of your body. If your body is not aligned with the compass, your course will not be accurate and you will not reach your destination.

If you wear your compass on your wrist, you can use what is known as the "compass lock position" to achieve greater accuracy in swimming your course. To use the compass lock position, if the compass is worn on your left forearm, extend your right arm out in front of you straight away from your body. Clasp your right elbow with your left hand so that your left arm is at a 90-degree angle. Be sure the compass is aligned with the long axis of your body before you start to swim your course.

It is difficult to look down at the face of the compass to swim your course and watch where you are going at the same time. For this reason, most compasses today also feature a side window that allows you to view your heading while holding the compass out in front of you. You can watch the side window and site over the top of compass to swim your course.

If you are swimming a compass course for practice or part of your training, be sure to mark your start point with a buoy. As you swim the course, note if there are any cross currents pushing you to either side. If the visibility is sufficient, you should be able to watch the bottom and compensate for any cross current. If the visibility is poor, it is difficult to accurately compensate for cross currents. As you swim your course, be sure to take note of any distinctive terrain features that will help you verify that you are swimming

The most accurate way to use your compass is to mount it on your wrist and use the "compass lock position."

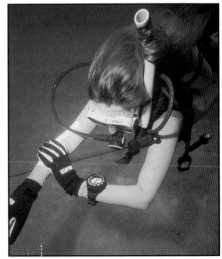

the correct reciprocal course on your return.

One of the difficulties that most people face in swimming a compass course is that most divers kick more strongly with one leg than the other. This tendency to kick harder with one leg will cause you to swim off to one side of your course or the other and must be compensated for to swim an accurate course.

Swimming a Reciprocal Course

Once you reach your target destination, immediately turn around so that you are facing exactly the direction from which you started. Do not turn the bezel when you change your course.

Planning a Navigation Exercise

If you want to practice your navigation skills, you will need two marker buoys in addition to your compass and other dive gear. You should plan your exercise for a site where you know the maximum depth.

Set the buoys up a distance of several hundred feet apart. Swim between the two buoys on the surface and see how long it takes to swim between them. If you have a watch or dive computer you can record the actual time. It should take roughly the same amount of time to swim between the buoys underwater.

If you find it difficult to check your computer and compass at the same time, you can count kick cycles to see how long it takes to swim the course. A kick cycle occurs each time your right leg reaches the bottom of its stroke. It should take roughly the same number of kick cycles to swim between the buoys underwater.

Starting at one of the buoys, take a bearing on the second buoy on the surface. Drop down to the bottom and align the lubber line with your body. When you and your dive partner are ready, start swimming the compass course. Time the course with your watch, or count kick cycles. When the time is up, or you have counted the correct number of kick cycles, you should be very close to the second buoy.

If you cannot see the second buoy, you should slowly surface and check your location. If you are far away from the target buoy, descend near the closest buoy, take a bearing on the distant buoy, and practice again. Eventually, you should get good enough so that you can swim from the first buoy to the second and back again without needing to surface.

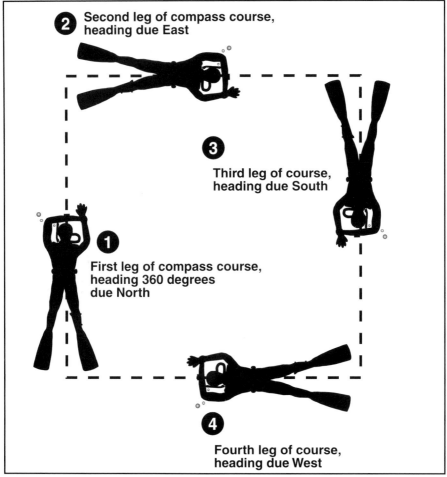

Bird's eye view of a diver swimming a "box" compass course.

Swimming a Box Course

Swimming a box course is only slightly different, but requires greater accuracy than swimming a reciprocal course. Use a marker buoy to mark the start of your box course.

When you swim a box course, you make three 90-degree turns in one direction. It doesn't matter which way you turn as long as all your turns are either to the left or to the right. At the completion of the box course, you should end up back at your starting point.

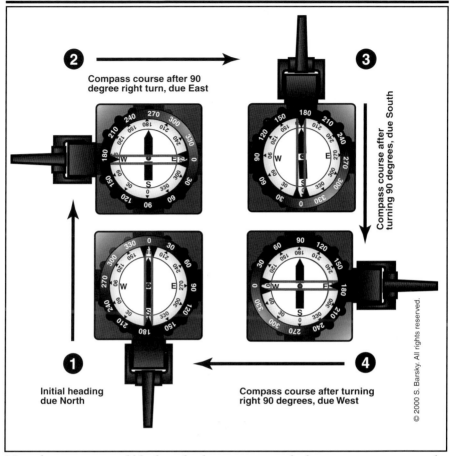

How the compass would look to the diver swimming the box compass course on the prior page.

Checking Your Position

If you do not have access to any electronic aids to navigation, and you did not reach your target underwater but you think you're close, you may need to swim several box courses to try to locate your target. This will usually only happen if the visibility is poor. If you have surface line-ups it will probably be quicker for you to surface and attempt to use your line-ups than to waste time underwater trying to find the site.

To try to locate your target underwater, the first box course you should swim should be in the general direction you think your target should be. Each leg of the box course should be short, not more than a minute per side, assuming your searching for a large dive site.

Locating small objects on the bottom, such as a pair of glasses or a wallet dropped over the side of the boat requires an entirely different set of skills, known as "search and recovery." To search for small objects you need to use "search patterns," which employ some of the skills of navigation but require different techniques.

Using an Electronic Compass

Using an electronic compass is a bit different from using a mechanical compass. With an electronic compass, there typically is no "lubber line," instead, the compass will usually give a reading in degrees only. When you point towards a target, you see the "bearing" or "course" in degrees.

Once you are pointed towards your target and have taken your bearing, you start swimming in that direction, while attempting to maintain the correct course. Most electronic compasses will feature a timer, too, so that you can time your swim. This is easier than trying to check a watch and a compass simultaneously, or counting kick cycles. Some electronic compasses can be set to lock your course heading into the system.

If you find that the compass shows that you have deviated from the correct course, you must change your heading until the compass displays the correct course again. Most electronic courses will show you which direction to swim, i.e., left or right, to correct your course

Once you have reached your destination, you are now ready to swim a reciprocal course. Your electronic compass will probably be equipped with a function that will automatically calculate a reciprocal course, which makes it

With an electronic compass, you will only see the heading in degrees.

easy to be certain you are following the correct path to your starting point. If the compass does not calculate a reciprocal for you, you simply need to turn around and note the new heading to swim back to your starting point. Most electronic compasses will also allow you to save a series of courses and plot the reciprocal courses for all of them with appropriate course changes.

Using an Underwater Tracking System

Electronic underwater tracking systems make underwater navigation easy. They are designed to help you locate a marked target, i.e., the sending unit or "transmitter," rather than for general navigation.

Underwater tracking systems operate over specific distances. The least powerful units will locate the sending unit (transmitter) at a distance of 1000 feet, while more powerful systems will be able to locate a transmitter at distances of up to 4000 feet. Most underwater tracking systems are designed for use in open water situations only, and do not perform properly in caves or when wrecks or reefs come between the transmitter and receiver. These are what we call "line-of-sight" systems, meaning there must be no large objects between the transmitter and receiver. The transmitter and receiver must be able to "see" each other.

Keep in mind that thermoclines, changes in salinity, a loss of battery power, and currents all can affect the accuracy and performance of a dive tracking system. Both the transmitter and the receiver must be working properly and communicating with each other. For this reason, you must never depend on a dive tracking system as your sole means of navigating underwater.

To use a dive tracking system, you activate the transmitter and place it in the water. If you are diving from a boat, you can hang the transmitter over

To use a dive tracking unit, you must hang the transmitter over the side of the boat, into the water. The receiver is held by the diver.

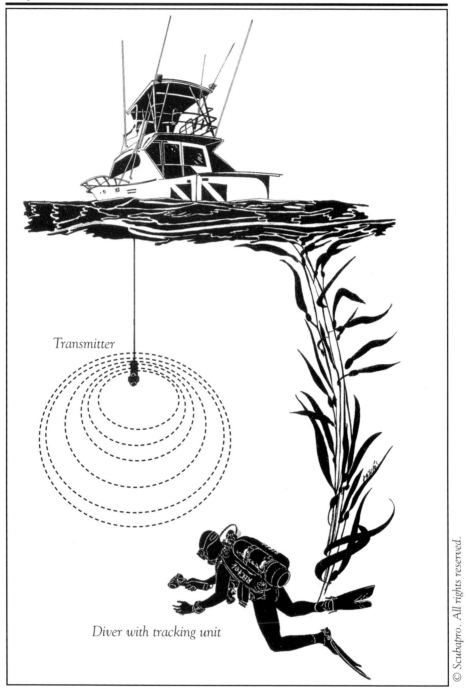

Transmitter

Diver with tracking unit

Like any diving skill, using a dive tracking device requires practice.

the side on a line, as long as it is at a depth sufficiently deeper than the hull, outdrive, or swimstep. Usually, a depth of about 10-15 feet is sufficient to avoid interference from the boat. However, you must be cautious if you are in shallow water and there are obstructions such as coral heads or wreckage, to avoid damaging the transmitter.

You can also attach the transmitter to the anchor line, which is frequently a better location, especially if you are diving in deep water and want to make your descent and ascent on the line. When the transmitter is hung over the side of the boat, returning to the boat underwater can be difficult if the boat swings through a wide arc with the wind. Depending on how much anchor line is out, the boat can change position by hundreds of feet very quickly, making your return difficult. With the transmitter on the anchor line near the bottom, even if the boat swings, the relative change in position of the transmitter will be small.

The transmitter should be attached at a point at least 10 feet above the bottom, to be sure that it will not hang up on any surrounding bottom structure. Never attach the transmitter directly to the anchor itself, as there is a good chance it will be damaged.

The easiest and most secure way to attach the transmitter to the anchor line is to connect it to the line using a lanyard by taking the lanyard around the line and passing the transmitter through the open end. You must ensure that the transmitter will not slip on the line and slide down to the bottom where it can be damaged.

Electronic navigation devices make finding your way underwater easy.

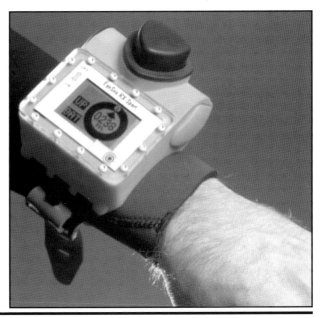

If you know how to tie a constrictor hitch or rolling hitch, these are more secure methods of fastening the line connected to the transmitter to the anchor line. If the anchor line is chain, you must fasten the transmitter in such a way that it does not bang against the chain as the boat rides up and down, or the transmitter can be damaged,

Prior to entering the water, connect the receiving unit (diver unit) to your buoyancy compensator using a retractor or lanyard. Some models may be worn on your wrist. The receiving unit does not need to be turned on until you are ready to use it, but depending on the type of system you are using, you may want to leave the receiver on at all times.

Some tracking systems will require you to be pointed in the correct direction, towards the transmitter, for the receiving unit to indicate not only the proper course, but also the distance to the transmitter. Sweep the receiver back and forth and you will see the direction where the signal is the strongest. Other systems will receive the signal no matter which direction you are pointed. Some systems also include a diver recall device, allowing topside to send a signal to the divers that they must return to the boat.

If you are using the transmitter to mark a wreck or a reef, you must place it high enough off the bottom that its signals will not be blocked by other obstructions. If you place the transmitter inside a wreck, you will not be able to home in on its signals.

Practice Your Navigation Skills Regularly

To be successful in underwater navigation you must use and practice your techniques frequently. You may not need to use your navigation skills to their fullest extent on a regular basis, especially if you normally dive in clear water. However, there may be times where proper navigation is crucial to your dive and your safety.

It is unreasonable to expect to be able to navigate correctly if you have done nothing to maintain your proficiency. Each member of the dive team should take turns navigating. It's much easier for one diver to observe the compass heading while the other diver looks after the details of depth and helping to avoid obstacles.

Scuba I.Q. Review

Prior to your first underwater navigation exercise, take the time to review this material with your instructor so you will be able to complete all of the exercises in the water successfully.

1) List the three different types of navigation that are available to the diver.

2) List three different physical features of the underwater environment that can be used to help you navigate during a dive and explain how they are used.

3) Using a mechanical compass, demonstrate how a bearing should be taken taken on dry land.

4) Define the term "reciprocal course."

5) Define the term "ferrous metal" and explain why this type of substance affects the accuracy of a compass. List one type of ferrous metal object a diver might encounter while diving.

6) Explain and demonstrate the "compass lock position."

7) Explain the term "line-of-sight" and how it affects the use of an underwater tracking system.

Chapter 5
Triangulation and Relocating Dive Sites

You're diving off the coast of Florida, on the last dive of the day with a charter operator in the Florida keys. As you and your buddy are swimming back to the boat, you spot something shiny sticking out of the sand. You swim down through a school of yellow striped fish and there on the bottom is a gold coin! You pick it up and can immediately tell that it is old, hundreds of years old, and you recognize the words on it as Spanish. It's a gold coin from some lost treasure galleon!

You show the coin to your buddy, tuck it into your glove, complete your precautionary decompression stop, and return to the boat. Back at the boat, the two of you can barely contain your excitement, but keep your secret to yourselves. You ask the captain the name of the dive site and he tells you it doesn't really have a name. As the boat crew pulls the anchor to head for the harbor, you look towards shore to try to pick out some recognizable landmarks so you can relocate the site, but you don't know which ones to choose. Will you ever be able to find the site again?

When you've located a new dive site and want to be able to return to it without using any instruments or electronics, triangulation is the method divers use to get themselves back to the same location. This method is so reliable and precise that it is possible to get back onto exactly the same spot with virtually no effort.

Triangulation is especially useful if you beach dive on a regular basis, or if you are diving from a boat that is not equipped with Loran or a GPS receiver. If you're diving from a boat and your electronics are inoperable, triangulation is the most reliable method for relocating a site.

What is Triangulation?

Triangulation is a navigation technique used by divers and boat operators to relocate an exact spot anywhere on the water, although the approach could just as easily be used on dry land. The technique consists of selecting a series of three pairs of landmarks on shore that are visible on the water and that have a spread of at least 90 degrees between any two adjacent pairs. When all three pairs are properly aligned you should find yourself directly over your target.

You can get by with only two sets of landmarks, but you will not have the same accuracy that occurs with three sets of bearings. Always try to get three sets of bearings whenever possible.

How Does Triangulation Work?

Each individual set of landmarks will consist of one object that is nearer to the water and lower than the second object that is further away and higher on shore. The best landmarks are permanent structures that are tall and relatively "thin," such as telephone poles, antennas, smokestacks, flagpoles, and similar items. You can also use the edge of a building, a chimney on a building, a window, a fence post, or other structures. Just be sure that you use objects that are "permanent," and not items that are likely to "move," such as the end of a temporary fence at a construction site.

Each pair of objects must align themselves so that when you are in the correct position over your dive site, one object from each pair appears to be directly above the other object in the same pair. All three pairs must line up in the proper orientation at the same time. If they don't you are not in the correct position.

To use triangulation properly, you must have a slate with you in the water to write down the information on the landmarks you are using to relocate your site. You need to draw a simple, but accurate sketch of how the landmarks align themselves, and make enough notes on the sketch that you will remember what you were using for your points of reference.

If you accidentally discover a good site and you don't have a slate with you, spend a few moments on the surface and try to memorize your lineups before you return to shore.

Make a sketch of your lineups as soon as possible so you don't forget them. At the end of your diving day, you'll want to make a copy of your sketch for your logbook so that you have a permanent record of how to relocate the dive site. If it is a particularly good site, you will probably want to do a detailed sketch and you may want to laminate it so that you can take it with you in the water.

If you buoyed the site and you're diving from a small boat that is not equipped with GPS, you may want to take photographs of the landmarks and how they line up. If you use this technique, you should still make an accurate sketch so that you can mark your lineups in the photos when you make prints

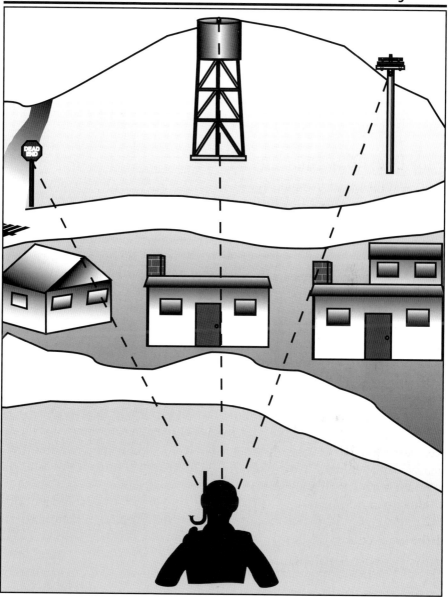

Triangulation as viewed from the diver's perspective. On the left, the line-ups are the peak of the house and the road sign. In the middle, the line-ups are the right side of the door frame of the house and the center of the water tower. On the right, the line-ups are the left edge of the roof and the pole.

All of the line-ups must be in position at the same time for the triangulation to work. If they are not in alignment, you must move either closer or further from the beach, or to your right or left.

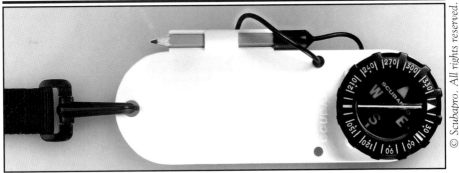

For triangulation, you'll need to have a slate with you in the water.

from your negatives, slides, or digital files. It's a good idea to keep your photos in a binder with plastic page protectors so that you can take it with you to the beach or on the boat the next time you go diving. If you follow this procedure, you'll end up with a book of valuable diving locations.

You can use triangulation at night, too, although admittedly, this is usually more difficult than during daylight hours. Landmarks that work well at night include streetlights, lighted antenna poles, lighthouses, and other objects that are similarly easy to see after dark.

Returning to a Triangulated Site

Returning to a triangulated site is a relatively simple process. Once you are in the water in the approximate vicinity of the dive site, position yourself so that the two most easily identifiable landmarks are in approximate alignment. Keeping the first two objects in relative alignment, you will need to swim either in towards shore or away from shore until the other two sets of objects line up. When all three sets of landmarks are in the position indicated by your sketch, you should be directly over the dive site.

Why Triangulation Sometimes Fails

Although triangulation is a great technique for relocating dive sites, sometimes you'll find that when you try to return to a site, your lineups don't seem to work. There are several reasons why it may not work, and if you know the problems, you can usually deal with them.

Most of the problems that occur with triangulation are a result of a failure on the diver's part to select, identify, and document good landmarks. For example, if you fail to maintain a fixed position when you take your initial bearings, you will find it impossible to relocate the dive site.

Try to use your line-ups from the same elevation for the greatest accuracy.

A frequent mistake made by beginning divers is to select landmarks that are too close together. Ideally, the spread between any two adjacent pairs of landmarks should be 90 degrees, but this may not always be possible. If the spread of your landmarks is not wide enough and if you have only two pairs of landmarks, this will further degrade your ability to get back on top of the site.

If you fail to carefully sketch the relationship between your landmarks you may also have a difficult time returning to the site. Be sure to make as detailed a sketch as possible so that you don't forget what the symbols in your drawing mean.

You should also use your line-ups from the same elevation for them to be the most accurate. If you record your original line-ups in the water, but try to get on the site again using the same line-ups from the deck of a boat, you may not get on the site precisely.

Factors that are beyond your control that may affect your ability to return to a previously identified site include the presence of fog and the removal of landmarks. Dense fog can make it difficult or impossible to see structures on land, rendering the use of triangulation impractical. When land is developed or old buildings are torn down to make room for new construction, landmarks that you may have previously used may disappear.

Practice Triangulation to Achieve Accuracy

Like any other skill, the more you practice triangulation, the better the accuracy you will achieve. This is a skill that every diver should know.

Scuba I.Q. Review

The capability to triangulate the location of a dive site is part of the package of skills you should possess to be competent in underwater navigation. You should be prepared to discuss the principles of triangulation with your instructor.

1) Define the term "triangulation."

2) List three items that make good landmarks for triangulation during the day.

3) State the one diving accessory that is essential for performing triangulation.

4) List three items that make good landmarks for triangulation at night.

5) Explain two reasons why triangulation sometimes fails.

6) State the minimum spread in degrees that there should be between adjacent sets of landmarks used in triangulation.

Notes:

Chapter 6
Night Diving

Night diving is popular in many areas, but especially so in the tropics and in areas like Southern California, where it is legal to night dive for lobsters. Although most divers find it somewhat "spooky" the first time they dive at night, you will find that you will quickly become comfortable with the experience and eagerly look forward to it.

As noted earlier in this book, a night dive is any dive that occurs between half an hour before sunset and half an hour before sunrise.

Rigging Your Gear for the Night Dive

Preparing your gear for night diving is relatively simple, however, it must be done correctly. Most of your gear will probably be ready to go, but you should double check to be sure each item is configured properly.

For night diving, be sure to check that both of your dive lights have fresh batteries and are operating properly. The o-ring that seals the light should be clean and lightly greased with silicone grease. Each light should be weighted for negative buoyancy and should be equipped with a lanyard or fastened to your BC with a retractor. Smaller back-up lights can go inside the pocket of your buoyancy compensator, but should be fastened into the pocket in some way so that they are not lost if the pocket accidentally comes open.

Every diver on the night dive must be equipped with either a chemical or battery powered light stick or marking light. The light stick can be attached to the top of your snorkel using waterproof electrical tape. It can also be attached to the first stage of your regulator, but this position is not as effective or safe as on the snorkel.

When the light stick is mounted on the first stage it can be more difficult to see underwater. Also, since the most common way to mount the light stick on the first stage is to tie it on with string, this creates the possibility of entanglement. The preferred mounting location for the light stick is on the snorkel. Chemical light sticks should always be disposed of properly and not left floating in the ocean after the dive.

Most dive computers and electronic pressure gauges are equipped with some type of backlighting system. Be sure you know how to operate the light in your system and that it is working properly before the dive.

Some manufacturers use other instrument lighting options. Some gauge faces are "luminescent" by themselves and emit a glow that can be seen in dark conditions. Other designs use a "light gathering" display that can be "charged" by holding a dive light against it for a few seconds. The gauge face will "absorb" and hold this light and be easy to read for quite some time after.

Once you have completed your night diver training, you may want to use your camera on a night dive. You can attach a small dive light to the underwater flash on your camera to help you see at night.

As in all diving, the use of an alternate air source is essential on a night dive, and an independent back-up supply is highly recommended. Just as it is more difficult to share air when the visibility is limited, sharing air on a night dive can be more difficult, too.

Whether you are diving from a boat or from shore, always be sure to rig an exit light whenever you are night diving. Depending on where you dive, different types of exit lights may be appropriate.

Any dive computer that you use should be equipped with a back-light system so that it can be easily read in the dark.

If you are diving from a boat, the boat will have an anchor light so that other boats in the area can see it. This is required by U.S. Coast Guard regulations in the United States. Although the anchor light will help you to find the boat on the surface, an exit light attached to the anchor line underwater is a wise idea. With an exit light attached to the anchor line a few feet below the surface, you can avoid the need to surface to locate the boat at the end of your dive, provided the visibility is good.

The most effective type of exit light for mounting on an anchor line is a waterproof strobe that flashes in all directions. An ordinary flashlight is not nearly as effective, since you will have a difficult time seeing the light unless it is pointed in your direction.

For marking a beach site, you can use a colored marking light, a flashing light, or any other type of light that will help you to distinguish your exit point. If you are diving an area where there is a shallow reef or other obstructions between you and shore, you may need to set up at least two lights to form a "range" to direct you to the correct path to follow out of the water back to the beach.

The exit lights must be in proper alignment for you to exit the water safely. The simplest range is composed of two lights that are on poles stuck in the sand at different heights, spaced at least five feet apart. Test any range you design during daylight hours so that you know what it looks like when you are out in the water.

If you are diving near a harbor or other area where there are navigational buoys with flashing lights, you must not use a flashing light for your exit light. If a boat operator mistakes your exit light for a navigational buoy, you could be held responsible if the boat goes aground or other boating accident occurs due to the placement of your light.

Be sure to test the operation of your whistle or air powered horn before you enter the water.

Planning Your Night Dive

The first step in planning any night dive is to select a spot that you know well. If you are diving a new location, you must take the time to dive the spot during daylight hours so that you become familiar with it.

During your daytime dives at the site, look for any prominent features that will help you to navigate and know where you are underwater. It's a good idea to make a simple sketch of the site on your underwater slate to help you keep the site in perspective.

When you select an area for night diving, be sure to pick a site with a minimum amount of boat traffic and with no strong currents. Even with a

If you are diving from a beach, you'll want to set up a "range" with lights to guide you back to the exit point. The range should be set up during daylight hours so that you can see where the lights are located. When the lights are in the proper alignment, you can swim up onto the beach, if all other conditions are safe.

light stick attached to your snorkel, it can be difficult for a boat operator to see you at night. If you are swept away by a current, it may be difficult for you to get the attention of the boat operator if seas are rough. In this situation a sound signaling device can be invaluable. If you are diving from shore and you are carried away from your exit point by a current, you may not be able to see the shore well enough to make a safe exit at another location.

Plan your underwater route carefully, taking into account any distinctive features or hazards of the site. You should also be conservative in your air usage and save a bit of air for emergency situations. How much extra air will depend on visibility, the depth of your dive, currents, and other environmental factors.

Avoid making night dives where the visibility is less than ten feet underwater.

Making the Night Dive

The first thing to do before you make your night dive is to take the time to mark your exit point. If you're diving from the beach, set up your lights on shore. If you're diving from a boat, connect the exit light to the anchor line and slack off enough additional line so that the light is below the surface of the water. Rig your light stick, don your gear, do your buddy checks, and prepare to enter the water.

Beach divers should always take a compass heading facing inland so they will be able to orient towards shore if fog should develop while they are

Check the operation of your dive lights before you enter the water, as part of your buddy checks. This diver is using a head mounted light as his primary dive light.

One technique that divers can use to help stay together during a night dive is for only one partner to operate his light at a time.

underwater. Dive tracking devices are extremely helpful in relocating the boat during a night dive.

If you are diving from a private boat, you should be using a current line with a float attached to the end of it, in the event that you surface down current behind the boat. On a night dive, your current line should also be marked with some type of light to that you can see it if you need to use it.

Once you and your partner are in the water, you can begin your descent. It is much easier to make your descent on the anchor line as this will give you a reference and help control your descent, particularly if you are having any difficulty with equalization. If you do use the anchor line for descent, avoid looking at the anchor line marking light as it will interfere with your night vision. Be sure to maintain good control of your buoyancy and avoid kicking as you near the bottom to help avoid stirring up any silt, further reducing visibility.

One technique that some divers use to help them stay together during a night dive is for only one member of the dive team to operate their light at a time. With only one light illuminating the bottom, the diver whose light is off won't stray far from the area that is lit! At all times avoid shining your light into your own or your dive partner's eyes.

We use special techniques for communicating during a night dive. When you are next to your buddy underwater, you can shine your light at your hand

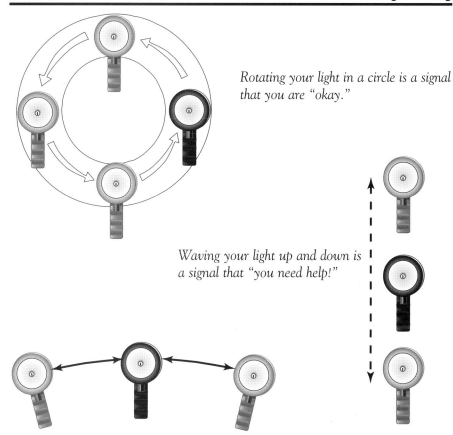

Rotating your light in a circle is a signal that you are "okay."

Waving your light up and down is a signal that "you need help!"

Swinging your light back and forth from side to side means that you "need attention."

and use any of your normal hand signals for communicating during the dive. At a distance, you can swing your light to communicate the following messages:

- Okay!
Rotate your light in a circle to indicate you are okay.
- I'm in distress! I need help!
Raise and lower your light vertically
- I need your attention!
Swing your light from side to side.

You must be proficient in your buoyancy control to ascend in mid-water. Here, divers can be seen ascending in clear water, at the stern of the boat. Whenever possible, ascend on the anchor line.

Ascending from a Night Dive

You must be proficient in your buoyancy control to ascend in mid-water without a reference during a night dive. Without good buoyancy control, it's very easy to ascend too quickly. Rapid ascents are potentially dangerous.

Whenever possible, you should attempt to ascend on the anchor line or by following the bottom contour. If this is not possible, you must monitor your dive computer carefully as you slowly ascend. Be sure to look up and shine your light overhead so that you can see any obstructions that may be on the surface above you. With your light pointed towards the surface, it is also more likely that any passing boat traffic will see it and avoid hitting you.

Night Diving Emergencies

Emergencies at night are usually more difficult to deal with than during the daytime due to the difficulty in seeing exactly what's happening. For this reason, good dive planning becomes even more important than during a daylight dive.

The loss of a primary or secondary dive light is a serious situation, that while not life-threatening, must not be casually dismissed. Whether you "lose" your light because it is physically lost, the batteries have died, or the bulb has burned out, you need to deal with the situation promptly. In any situation where you have lost one of your lights, your dive should be terminated as soon as possible. You don't need to panic over this, but you do need to get out of the water until you can "replace" your light.

Buddy separation is another common problem that can occur during a night dive, particularly if visibility is not high. In any case of buddy separation you want to scan the area immediately around you for not more than a minute and then surface to link up with your dive partner again. Do not submerge again until you have positively located your buddy.

If your air supply should fail during a night dive, this is a more serious problem than during a daytime dive simply due to the fact that it is more difficult to see things that are not directly illuminated at night. You must always know the exact location of your dive partner's octopus rig. Better yet, carry an independent alternate air source.

In temperate areas, one of the hazards of night diving is the possibility of fog occurring before or during a night dive. If it seems likely that fog will occur, you should postpone your dive, since relocating the boat or shore can be extremely difficult in foggy conditions. Should fog occur while you are underwater, you may surface and be unable to see your exit point.

If you are near shore when fog occurs, it is usually possible to locate the shore by the sound of the surf or by using your compass. Boat divers who are a distance from shore may find it extremely difficult to relocate the boat visually. To signal to the boat, use your sound signaling device and listen for a reply from the crew aboard the boat before you start swimming. You may need to blow your whistle or air horn more than once as you swim back to the boat on the surface to get a reply from the boat to help keep you on course.

Scuba I.Q. Review

Prior to your first night dive, review the procedures for the dive with your instructor by discussing the questions listed below.

1) State the preferred location to fasten your light stick and the alternate location.

2) State the preferred location for your exit light for night diving operations from a boat.

3) List two important factors in selecting a site for a night dive.

4) Explain why it is important to take a compass heading facing toward shore

before leaving the beach when making a night dive from shore.

5) Explain the proper technique for using hand signals at night underwater.

6) Describe the three standard diving signals that can be made using a light at a distance at night.

7) Explain three conditions that would cause you to terminate a night dive.

Notes:

Chapter 7
Limited Visibility Diving

Underwater visibility is defined as the distance that you can see in any single direction underwater. In most cases, if you are looking up towards the surface during daytime hours, you may be able to see objects that are further away than those that are at the same depth as you. In reality, what you are seeing when you look upwards is the contrast between the object and the surrounding water as the object is struck by light from above (backlighting).

Most divers are poor at estimating underwater visibility unless they are involved in underwater photography and must estimate distance in order to set their camera. The fact that objects underwater appear larger and closer can make it difficult for the beginning diver to estimate distances.

Limited visibility is a relative term. If you normally dive in the Florida Keys, where the visibility is usually at least 75 feet or more, then you might consider the visibility to be poor when you can only see for 20 feet underwater. However, if you regularly dive in Monterey, California, where the visibility averages 15-20 feet, then you might think that visibility of less than 10 feet is poor.

Limited visibility can be caused by many environmental and man-made factors. These include high surf, run-off from storms, plankton, and pollution. In the rivers, streams, and springs of Florida, tannic acid from vegetation can severely reduce visibility at certain times of the year.

For argument's sake, we consider limited visibility to occur any time the visibility is less than six feet. If you live in an area where the visibility never gets this low, consider yourself lucky!

Avoid Zero Visibility Conditions

Occasionally, even in good dive areas, the visibility will become so poor, less than a foot, that for all practical purposes we say that the visibility is "zero." Diving in these conditions becomes very hazardous and should be avoided by sport divers.

Commercial divers and professionals who dive for law enforcement, science, or other professions may need to dive in zero visibility conditions for their work. However, generally speaking, there is no reason for a recreational diver to dive when they cannot see.

When Should You Consider Diving in Limited Visibility?

There are occasions when sport divers may want or need to dive in conditions where the visibility is limited. Such situations might include the recovery of an item that has been lost underwater, to perform a rescue, or when technical divers enter wrecks or caves. In certain areas, limited visibility diving may be the only diving conditions available for certain periods each year.

Hazards of Limited Visibility Diving

There are several serious hazards in limited visibility diving that you must take into consideration whenever you plan a limited visibility dive. The most common is the danger of entanglement. When the visibility is poor, it is extremely easy to become entangled in fishing nets, monofilament fishing line (which tends to be transparent underwater), and other similar dangers.

Two other common hazards in limited visibility diving are buddy separation and becoming lost or disoriented. There are several specific techniques for avoiding buddy separation in limited visibility that we will discuss later in this chapter.

By using the underwater navigation skills discussed earlier in this book, you can help avoid becoming lost when the visibility is limited. Navigation becomes more difficult in limited visibility because it is easier to miss underwater landmarks when the visibility is restricted. If an object that you would normally see while en route to your dive site is usually eight feet away from the course you usually swim, but the visibility is only seven feet, you will not see the object and could become confused about your location.

Diving around shipwrecks in limited visibility exposes you to the possibility that you may unknowingly "penetrate" or enter the wreck without realizing it. In this situation you may find yourself without a clear ascent path to the surface. This is known as diving in an "overhead environment" and requires additional specialized training which is beyond the scope of this course.

Another potential hazard of limited visibility diving that most divers fail to consider is that there may be an important reason why the visibility is reduced. For example, following heavy rains it is common for sewage systems to overflow, dumping raw sewage into ocean waters. If the water looks "bad"

If the visibility is limited, you could accidentally enter a shipwreck without knowing it. Diving inside shipwrecks requires additional special training.

and smells "bad," it's a good idea to be cautious even if there are no signs present along the waterfront warning about contaminants in the water. However, even water that appears relatively "clean" and "clear" may contain bacterial or other pollutants that are invisible to the naked eye and give off no offensive smell. Diving in polluted water is extremely dangerous and can expose you to life threatening or debilitating biological and/or chemical hazards.

Additional Equipment for Limited Visibility Diving

To help increase your safety in limited visibility, there are some additional pieces of equipment that you should consider adding to your gear. These items include additional knives, a pair of sidecutters, an independent back-up air supply, and a "buddy line."

In the event that you become entangled in rope during a limited visibility dive, a second knife can be an invaluable tool. Having a second knife could mean the difference between easily dealing with entanglement or finding yourself in a real emergency. There are two primary situations where a second knife is of great value; if you lose your knife or if your primary knife becomes dull. There are a number of compact diving knives on the market today that can be mounted on a gauge hose or on a buoyancy compensator, making equipping yourself with a second knife quite easy.

Any time you dive in limited visibility, it's a good idea to carry a second dive knife.

Sidecutters (lineman's pliers) are another type of tool that can make releasing yourself from entanglement much simpler. Sidecutters are the only good way to cut wire and are more efficient for cutting monofilament than most knives.

If you must dive in limited visibility on a regular basis, you should seriously consider the addition of an independent back-up air supply. In the event that you become separated from your buddy, and your air supply should fail, an independent air supply could save your life. An independent back-up air supply consists of a separate smaller scuba cylinder equipped with its own regulator. The size of the cylinder is dependent on the depth to which you are diving. An optimal size cylinder for most situations is a 13 cubic foot cylinder.

These small scuba cylinders are commonly referred to as "bail-out bottles." They are commonly attached to the diver's primary cylinder by means of a small bracket.

A buddy line is a short rope, usually made from 1/4 inch or 1/2 inch thick nylon, usually not more than three feet long, that can be used to help two divers stay together when diving in limited visibility. The line should have a loop in each end that is large enough to allow you to place your fingers through it to hold onto the loop. However, the line should never be passed all the way around the diver's wrist.

Lights are of little value in limited visibility diving. They will not help you to see any further in limited visibility, but they are of some value at deeper depths where sunlight will not penetrate. Using a light in limited visibility has the same effect as turning on your car's high beam headlights in fog.

It's a good idea to carry a complete-ly independent back-up air supply, like the Spare-Air™ that this diver is wearing on his waist. This type of back-up device is especially impor-tant in limited visibility.

For deeper dives or when there is a greater chance of entanglement, a larger bail-out bottle with a separate regulator can be rigged on the diver's cylinder. Ideally, the bail-out bottle should be rigged to provide the lowest profile possible for better balance and to help avoid additional possibilities for entanglement.

The light doesn't penetrate the water but is reflected back at you by the suspended matter in the water.

Planning the Limited Visibility Dive

Your planning for a limited visibility dive should be much more conservative than for most other types of diving. The risks for a limited visibility dive are greater than for ordinary sport dives.

One of the techniques that should be used for planning a limited visibility dive is to be more cautious regarding your air supply. One method of planning your dive that you should consider is known as the "Rule of Thirds." This is a technique that is commonly used by cave and wreck divers.

The "Rule of Thirds" states that you should plan your dive so that you use one third of your air for reaching the objective of your dive and for accomplishing whatever it is you set out to do. The second third of your air supply should be reserved for returning from your objective to the surface. Finally, the last third of your air supply should be reserved for emergencies.

Be sure to avoid areas with strong currents when diving in limited visibility. A current can carry you towards hazards you will not see until you are right on top of them.

Before you enter the water for a limited visibility dive, both you and your dive partner must agree on what conditions will cause you to terminate the dive. If either diver reaches a point where they feel their safety is being compromised, the dive should be terminated immediately.

It is not uncommon for divers to feel nervous about diving in limited visibility. A little bit of nervous tension is acceptable and helps to heighten your awareness. However, if either diver reaches a point where they feel uncomfortable, there should be no penalty or argument about terminating or aborting a dive before it has begun.

1/3 for the job

1/3 for exiting water

1/3 for emergencies

The Rule of Thirds states that you should plan your dive so that you use one third of your air for reaching your objective and making the dive, one third of your air for returning to the surface, and reserve one third of your air for emergencies. This is a good practice in limited visibility diving.

Divers sometimes hold hands in limited visibility to help them stay together.

Hand Signals and Line Signals

Diving in limited visibility also means that you may not always be able to use traditional hand signals, particularly when the visibility is less than two feet. If the visibility is low and the water is cold, you may need to wear thick gloves or mittens that can further reduce your ability to use hand signals effectively.

You may find that you need to hold your hand right up to your buddy's face, or you may need to use "tactile" hand signals to convey specific messages. Instead of making a thumbs up sign to signal that you want to go up, you may need to hold your hand with your thumb indicating "up" against your buddy's palm. If you are going to use tactile hand signals, you need to decide what these signals will be and how you will use them before you get in the water. These signals must be practiced before you get in the water.

Sometimes the easiest way for dive partners to stay together in limited visibility is for the two divers to either hold hands or use a "buddy line." If you hold hands you may want to agree on a series of hand squeezes to use as a set of signals. Similarly, if you use a buddy line you should have a series of line pull signals agreed upon before you get in the water. Any signals you decide to use must be practiced before you get in the water.

One of the difficulties in using a buddy line is that in certain situations the line may make it difficult for you to maneuver. For example, if you are diving in a kelp bed, a buddy line is not a practical solution for two divers to

Using a buddy line is another technique that divers use to stay together in limited visibility.

remain in contact, since each time you encounter a kelp plant, both divers will either need to go around it on the same side, or one diver must release the buddy line and pass it around the kelp. In situations like this, it may be more practical for the divers to hold hands.

If you use wireless communications with a full-face mask you still need to maintain good buddy contact.

Limited Visibility Diving Techniques

Divers who partner together on a regular basis will undoubtedly develop their own special techniques for limited visibility diving, but there are general procedures for this type of dive that are commonly followed. Above all, cautious and deliberate movements are required for this type of diving.

As in any diving where two divers are attempting to stay together, maintaining a consistent physical orientation during the dive will go a long way toward avoiding buddy separation. One buddy should always remain on the left side while the other partner remains on the right. If you constantly switch sides, or one partner lags behind the other, it is extremely easy to get separated.

If you regularly do underwater photography, or you dive with a photographer, you know how upset someone can get when another diver stirs up the bottom. In limited visibility, neutral buoyancy and proper trim become more important than they are in ordinary situations. During a limited visibility dive, both divers should strive to swim with a slight head down attitude, so that their feet are slightly higher than their head. This will help to avoid stirring up any more sediment than is already in the water.

Emergencies in Limited Visibility Diving

The most serious emergency in limited visibility diving is entanglement, especially if the entanglement is caught on your tank valve or first stage. If this occurs, the first thing you must do is to stop all movement and allow your dive partner to assist you in sorting out the problem. If you thrash about you will generally only make the problem worse.

Entanglement becomes more serious if you have separated from your dive partner. If you have plenty of air, and you are confident in your partner's ability to find and assist you, it is essential to relax and slow your breathing while you wait for assistance.

If you are entangled and your dive partner does not come to assist you within a reasonable period of time, no more than five minutes, AND you have plenty of air, it is time to think about carefully removing your scuba unit so you can free yourself. If your air supply is low, however, you must not hesitate to remove your scuba unit to free yourself. This is where a completely independent back-up air supply becomes invaluable.

In situations where you are not entangled, but find yourself separated from your dive partner, do a 360-degree sweep on the bottom. If you do not see your partner within one minute, you should immediately surface. If you surface and do not see your partner within another minute, you should begin to search for their bubbles on the surface. If you still cannot locate them, you should summon assistance rather than attempt to locate them yourself underwater.

All skills that involve coordination between two diving partners become more difficult in limited visibility. In fact, any skill that requires you to see is more difficult when the visibility is restricted. For this reason, it is essential to be able to perform any task that you must do underwater completely by feel.

Ascents in Limited Visibility

When the water is clear, it is only necessary to look up and turn a slow spiral through the water to make sure that you do not ascend underneath a boat or other object. However, when the visibility is poor, it is critical that you not only look up, but also reach up with your hand over your hand, to avoid hitting any large objects with your head.

When the visibility is limited, it also becomes much more difficult to complete a hovering precautionary decompression stop in mid-water. Without a point of reference, it is difficult to maintain a constant depth when you only have your computer to check your depth. It is much easier to maintain your depth when there is something to see, such as a kelp plant, that allows you to maintain a constant position relative to it. In limited visibility, the preferred technique for ascending is to use the anchor line, or to follow the bottom contour back to shallower water.

Scuba I.Q. Review

Diving in limited visibility can be intimidating at first, but with a bit of practice and the help of your instructor, you'll find out there is nothing difficult about it. Discuss these limited visibility diving techniques with your instructor.

1) Define the term "limited visibility diving."

2) Define the term "zero visibility."

3) List two situations where a diver may need to dive in limited visibility.

4) State two common hazards in limited visibility diving.

5) List three pieces of equipment that are helpful in limited visibility diving.

6) Explain why an underwater light is of little use in limited visibility.

7) Explain the "rule of thirds" and how it is applicable to diving in limited visibility.

8) Explain the most serious emergency situation that could occur in limited visibility diving.

9) Explain why making a hovering precautionary decompression stop is difficult when the visibility is limited underwater.

Notes:

Chapter 8
Extending Your Diving Capabilities

With the completion of your training in night diving, underwater navigation, and limited visibility diving, your confidence in your diving abilities and knowledge should increase greatly. Yet these courses are just a small part of the world of diving and there is much more to learn to become a truly proficient diver. Additional training that you need to round out your diving education include the following:

- Nitrox diving
- Deep diving
- Boat diving
- Wreck diving
- Computer diving
- Technical diving
- Rescue diving

Nitrox Diving

Nitrox is a gas mixture that contains nitrogen and oxygen in proportions other than what is normally found in ordinary air. It is more properly referred to as enriched air nitrox, since these mixtures commonly contain more oxygen and less nitrogen than regular air.

By increasing the amount of oxygen in the gas mixture, it is possible to increase your maximum allowable bottom time at any given depth without requiring decompression. Nitrox is beneficial to all divers who want to stay underwater for longer periods of time, but is especially appreciated by underwater photographers, wreck divers, and cavern divers. Underwater scientists commonly use nitrox to allow them more bottom time to get their work done.

Nitrox can greatly extend your diving capabilities. Nitrox diving requires additional training.

The SDI Easy Nitrox Course will get you diving with nitrox without the need to learn complex mathematical formulas. The program is designed to allow you to dive with nitrox by using a dive computer using gas mixtures that contain as much as 40% oxygen.

Deep Diving

Deep diving training prepares you to explore dive sites at depths between 60 and 130 feet of seawater. By itself, diving deep has no purpose, but when you have something to see or do at deeper depths, the capability to do this properly is important.

Deep diving training includes the selection and preparation of equipment for this type of diving, diving procedures and precautions, detailed information on decompression, and much more. During the course, you have the opportunity to make progressively deeper dives under the direct supervision of an instructor. The student to instructor ratio is kept low for maximum safety and learning.

Deep diving training is crucial to anyone who wants to fully participate in all aspects of diving.

Deep diving training will provide you with techniques for diving to a maximum depth of 130 FSW.

Computer Diving

If you started your diver training with Scuba Diving International, you learned how to use a dive computer, starting with your initial diver training. But, there is much more to using a dive computer than just turning it on and diving with it.

In the computer diving course, you'll gain a deeper appreciation for what makes a dive computer work, the theory behind its operation, and how to get the most out of the dive planning and dive log functions. You'll also get the opportunity to look at the differences between dive computers so that you have a better understanding of why different types of computers provide different profiles for the same dive.

Boat Diving

There's no substitute for boat diving if you want to explore remote diving locations. Although boat diving is simple, there are many things that you can do to make your boat diving adventures more comfortable and enjoyable.

Boat diving training will help to prepare you for diving from many different types of boats, from small inflatables through luxury dive boats. You'll learn the best methods for entry and exits for all types of boats, how to properly pack and stow your gear, as well as the procedures and proper etiquette for this type of diving.

In the boat diving course, you will learn techniques for dive boats of all sizes.

Since most divers do a good portion of their diving from boats, this course is considered essential.

Wreck Diving

Exploring shipwrecks is one of the most exciting parts of diving and the SDI Wreck Diving course helps to prepare you to experience this adventure. Whether it's exploring a sunken galleon or a tramp steamer from World War II, few dives hold more mystery or thrills.

Wreck diving training will familiarize you with the specialized techniques for diving shipwrecks in different environments. Since not all wrecks are intact, you'll learn how to view a wreck with an eye towards understanding the layout of the ship on the bottom. You'll also learn how to avoid hazards, rig your gear, and how to research a wreck and its history.

Rescue Diving

In your initial diver training course, you learned the fundamentals of self-rescue and basic methods of assisting a diver in distress. However, have you ever considered what would happen if you had to rescue another diver by yourself in a remote location? How would you handle this type of situation without the proper training?

Rescue diver training is designed to give you the capability to assist

Wreck diving is one of the most exciting activities in diving.

another diver in the event of a diving emergency. You will learn the techniques for assists and tows, as well as how to handle an unconscious diver both underwater and on the surface, as well as how to deal with a panicked diver.

Rescue diver training is the first step for anyone who intends to become a divemaster or diving instructor. If you dive in remote areas, where it's just you and your buddy, you need to know how to perform a diving rescue.

Technical Diving

Technical diving is a type of recreational diving that goes beyond the normal standards for sport diving. Most technical dives typically involve dives made beyond 130 FSW, dives that use gas mixtures that contain more than 40% oxygen, decompression dives, and dives in overhead environments where there is no direct access to the surface. Penetration wreck dives and cave dives are both considered forms of technical diving, as are dives using gas mixtures other than nitrox, such as helium and oxygen.

Technical diving requires a great deal of training, equipment, and experience. It is not for everyone, but for those divers who crave diving at the extremes, this is the path to unique adventures.

Scuba I.Q. Review

As you progress in your diving skills, you'll want to explore new types of diving. Discuss your abilities and interests with your instructor to determine which training course you should take next. Here are some questions that you should be able to answer to help determine your future in diving.

1) What is nitrox?

2) List two benefits that using nitrox provides the diver?

3) State the maximum depth limit for sport diving?

4) List two additional functions beside dive monitoring that are possible when using a dive computer?

5) Explain one reason why rescue diver training is important?

6) Define the term "technical diving?"

Notes:

Additional Reading

Barsky, S. *Diving in High-Risk Environments, 3rd Edition*. Hammerhead Press, Santa Barbara, CA, 1999, 197 pages

Maloney, S. and Chapman, C. Chapman *Piloting: Seamanship and Boat Handling, 63rd Edition*. Hearst Books, New York, NY, 1999, 656 pages

About TDI/SDI

About TDI

TDI was formed in 1994 by some of diving's most experienced instructors to bring technical applications of the sport to a wider audience. TDI's library of training materials and texts have become known as the industry's best and most professional resources. Most importantly, TDI has the best safety record of all training agencies.

Whether your interests lie in nitrox, rebreathers, mixed gas or any of the many other programs that TDI offers you can be assured that you will be participating in training that offers you the "cutting edge" of diving technology. With offices worldwide and over 10,000 instructors teaching our programs, TDI has become the largest international specialized dive agency.

About SDI

SDI grew out of the success of our sister company TDI, which specialized in more advanced disciplines of dive training. Our instructors asked for an entry level scuba training program that would reflect that same forward-looking approach that TDI brought to technical diving pursuits.

Finally after a year in development, the SDI training program was launched at the 1999 DEMA show. It was an instant success on its own merits. Both students and instructors have embraced the no nonsense approach that the SDI training system offers. We have streamlined the course materials to let students study the essential academics with a renewed emphasis on practical diving skills learned in both the pool and open water environments. And SDI was the first to require students to be taught with modern dive computers from the outset.

Diving is constantly changing. Many other agencies are still mired in yesterday while our staff looks ahead to the millennium and strives to continue our record as the innovators of the industry. We want to make the experience of diving one that is enjoyed by every family member to the fullest. As SDI we are all divers and want to share our love of the sport with as wide an audience as possible. Please check out the variety of programs at SDI and join us in our passion!

SDI DIVER PROGRAMS

SCUBA DIVING INTERNATIONAL

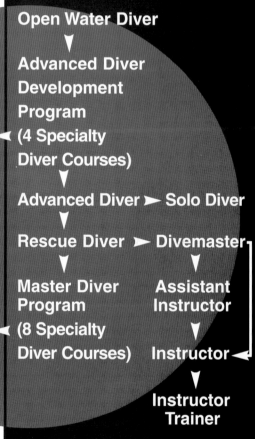

Open Water Diver
▼
Advanced Diver Development Program
(4 Specialty Diver Courses)
▼
Advanced Diver ► Solo Diver
▼
Rescue Diver ► Divemaster
▼   ▼
Master Diver Program   Assistant Instructor
(8 Specialty Diver Courses)   ▼
                        Instructor ◄
                             ▼
                        Instructor Trainer

- Altitude Diver
- Boat Diver
- Computer Diver
- Computer Nitrox Diver
- CPROX Administrator
- CPR1st Administrator
- Deep Diver(130ft Max)
- Diver Propulsion Vehicle
- Drift Diver
- Dry Suit Diver
- Equipment Specialist
- Ice Diver
- Marine Ecosystems Awareness
- Night/ Limited Visibility Diver
- Research Diver
- Search & Recovery Diver
- Shore/Beach Diver
- Underwater Navigation
- Underwater Photography
- Underwater Video
- Wreck Diver
- Underwater Hunter & Collector

Glossary

bail-out bottle: A small scuba cylinder designed to be attached to a diver's primary cylinder to serve as an independent back-up supply in the event the main supply is exhausted or the equipment fails.

buddy line: A line used by divers who are underwater in limited visibility as a means of staying together.

compass: A mechanical or electronic device that provides an aid to navigation by indicating the position of magnetic north. Based on the location of magnetic north, the user can than follow a route relative to its position.

compass lock position: A posture used by a diver to accurately swim a compass course underwater. With the compass mounted on the diver's left forearm, and the arm bent at a 90-degree angle in front of the diver, the diver grasps his right elbow with his left hand.

compass navigation: Using a compass to swim from one known point to another underwater.

Cyalume®: A plastic tube containing a chemical and an inner sealed glass tube containing a second chemical. When the plastic tube is bent, the glass tube breaks and the two chemicals mix, emitting light.

Dive-tracking device: An electronic system used by divers to navigate back to the boat or other site underwater. The system consists of a sending and receiving unit. The sender is attached to the anchor or other site. The diver uses the receiver to locate the sender and return to it.

exit light: A light used to mark the location of an anchor line or the beach.

fathometer: An electronic device used aboard a boat to measure the depth of water and bottom contour under the boat.

ferrous metal: Any metal that contains iron. Steel is a ferrous metal, but aluminum is not.

GPS: Global Positioning System. A system of satellites in orbit above the earth that send out electronic signals. The signals are read on earth by electronic receiver devices that calculate the distance between the satellites and receiver and plot the receiver's position on the face of the earth.

light stick: A small light that will provide 360-degree illumination. Used by divers to identify their location at night.

limited visibility: Conditions that exist underwater where a diver cannot see more than six feet in any one direction.

LORAN: Long Range Navigation system. A system of land based stations that transmit electronic signals that are captured by receiver devices. The signals are used to calculate the relative distance and direction of each station and calculate the location of the receiving device.

lubber line: A line on the face of a mechanical compass that the user aligns with the longitudinal axis of his body to help ensure he is following the correct course.

magnetic north: The spot on the earth to which all compasses will point.

natural navigation: Navigating underwater using physical features of the terrain and environment to determine your location. These features might include sand ripples, depth contour, wrecks, reefs, currents, and similar physical items.

night diving: Any dive that takes place 30 minutes after sundown or 30 minutes before sunrise.

reciprocal course: The course followed to return directly to your starting point underwater, after swimming a straight line in one direction. The reciprocal is determined by turning around and facing the exact direction from which you started. On a compass, the reciprocal course is 180 degrees opposite the course you were following on your outbound swim.

retractor: A mechanical device used to attach accessories to the diver's buoyancy compensator. The device contains a spring-loaded reel with a line attached to it. The accessory is clipped to the end of the line. When the accessory is needed, the diver pulls it away from the retractor and line automatically unreels. When the diver is done using the accessory and releases it, the retractor automatically reels the accessory back in.

rule of thirds: A procedure used for diving in hazardous situations. One third of the air supply is used for reaching the dive objective and making the dive, one third of the supply is used for exiting the water, one third of the supply is reserved for emergencies.

triangulation: A technique used to relocate an underwater site by taking bearings on structures or physical features on shore.

zero visibility: Diving conditions where the diver can see less than one foot in any direction.

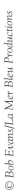

© *Bob Evans/La Mer Bleu Productions*

About the Author
Steven M. Barsky

Steve Barsky started diving in 1965 in Los Angeles County, and became a NAUI instructor in 1970. His first employment in the industry was with a dive store in Los Angeles and he went on to work for almost 10 years in the retail dive store environment.

Steve attended the University of California at Santa Barbara, where he earned a Masters Degree in 1976 in Human Factors/Ergonomics. This has helped greatly in his thorough understanding of diving equipment design and use. His master's thesis was one of the first to deal with the use of underwater video systems in commercial diving. His work was a pioneering effort at the time (1976) and was used by the Navy in developing applications for underwater video systems.

His background includes being a commercial diver, working in the offshore oil industry in the North Sea, Gulf of Mexico, and South America. He worked as both an air diving supervisor and a mixed gas saturation diver, making working dives down to 580'.

Barsky was marketing manager for Viking America, Inc., an international manufacturer of dry suits. He also served in a similar position at Diving Systems International (DSI), the world's leading manufacturer of commercial diving helmets.

Steve is an accomplished underwater photographer. His photos have been used in numerous magazine articles, catalogs, advertising, training programs, and textbooks.

About the Author

A prolific writer, Barsky's work has been published in *Sea Technology, Skin Diver, Offshore Magazine, Emergency, Fire Engineering, Dive Training Magazine, Searchlines, Sources, Undersea Biomedical Reports, Santa Barbara Magazine, Underwater Magazine*, and many other publications. He is the author of the *Dry Suit Diving Manual, Diving in High Risk Environments, Spearfishing for Skin and Scuba Divers, Small Boat Diving, Diving with the EXO-26 Full Face Mask, Diving with the Divator MK II Full Face Mask*, and a joint author with Dick Long and Bob Stinton of *Dry Suit Diving: A Guide to Diving Dry*. Steve has taught numerous workshops on contaminated water diving, dry suits, small boat diving, spearfishing, and other diving topics. *The Simple Guide to Rebreather Diving* was written by Steve along with Mark Thurlow and Mike Ward.

In 1989 Steve formed Marine Marketing and Consulting, based in Santa Barbara, California. The company provides market research, marketing plans, consulting, newsletters, promotional articles, technical manuals, and other services for the diving and ocean industry. He has consulted to Dräger, AquaLung/U.S. Divers Co., Inc, Zeagle Systems, Inc., Diving Unlimited Intnl., Diving Systems Intnl, DAN, NAUI, and numerous other companies. He also investigates diving accidents and serves as an expert witness in dive accident litigation.

In 1999, Steve and his wife Kristine formed Hammerhead Press to publish high quality diving books. Hammerhead Press is a subsidiary of the Carcharodon Corporation.

Steve is an instructor with SDI, TDI, NAUI, and PADI. You can purchase Steve's other books on-line at http://www.hammerheadpress.com/

Index